STEP
FORWARD
WITH

OPTIMISM

REAGAN MILLER

Crabtree Publishing Company

www.crabtreebooks.com

STEP FORWARD!

Dedicated by Larry Miller
To my dear granddaughter Bryley,
May your optimism lead you to great achievements!

Author
Reagan Miller

Series research and development
Reagan Miller

Editorial director
Kathy Middleton

Editor
Janine Deschenes

Series Consultant
Larry Miller: BA (Sociology), BPE, MSc.Ed
Retired teacher, guidance counselor, and certified coach

Print and production coordinator
Katherine Berti

Design and photo research
Katherine Berti

Photographs
Getty Images: Brian Vander Brug, p 9;
  Stephen J. Cohen, p 17
Shutterstock: © Sylvia sooyoN, p 7;
Other images by Shutterstock

Library and Archives Canada Cataloguing in Publication

Miller, Reagan, author
   Step forward with optimism / Reagan Miller.

(Step forward!)
Includes index.
Issued in print and electronic formats.
ISBN 978-0-7787-2780-4 (hardback).--
ISBN 978-0-7787-2822-1 (paperback).--ISBN 978-1-4271-1828-8 (html)

   1. Optimism--Juvenile literature. I. Title.

BF698.35.O57M555 2016   j155.2'32   C2016-903355-4
                                          C2016-903356-2

Library of Congress Cataloging-in-Publication Data

CIP Available at the Library of Congress

Crabtree Publishing Company
www.crabtreebooks.com   1-800-387-7650

Printed in Canada/102016/IH20160811

Published in Canada
Crabtree Publishing
616 Welland Ave.
St. Catharines, Ontario
L2M 5V6

Published in the United States
Crabtree Publishing
PMB 59051
350 Fifth Avenue, 59th Floor
New York, New York 10118

Published in the United Kingdom
Crabtree Publishing
Maritime House
Basin Road North, Hove
BN41 1WR

Published in Australia
Crabtree Publishing
3 Charles Street
Coburg North
VIC 3058

CONTENTS

WHAT IS OPTIMISM?

Optimism describes a positive **attitude, or way of feeling or thinking about something or someone.**

A person who has optimism is called an **optimist**. Optimists are hopeful that the situations they face will go well. They expect the best in the future and work hard to reach their **goals**. When faced with a problem or challenge, optimists focus on what they can do to improve the situation. They believe things will get better.

A person with a **negative** attitude is called a **pessimist**. When faced with a problem, pessimists are more likely to focus on what is wrong or unfair. They often feel helpless and unable to solve problems. They don't believe things will improve.

Optimism isn't something people are either born with or without. Everyone can learn to have a positive attitude. Just like learning anything new, it takes work and practice.

WHY IS OPTIMISM IMPORTANT?

Optimism is important because it helps you get past challenges and keep reaching for your goals.

Imagine you tried out for the school soccer team. You worked hard, had fun, and even learned some new skills. When the coach posts the list of the kids who made the team, your name is not on it. How would you react to this situation?

A

You decide that you are terrible at all sports and tell yourself you will never try out for any team again—ever.

B

You ask a friend who made the team to help you with your soccer skills over the summer. You want to be ready to try out again next year.

It is normal to feel disappointed in this kind of situation. The difference between an optimist and pessimist is how a person responds or reacts to a situation.

STEP FURTHER

Which option best describes how an optimist would react to not making the team?

Optimism is not just about hoping good things will happen. Optimists use positive thinking to make plans and take action to reach their goals—even when they feel disappointed about something.

Positive thoughts and feelings can make you feel more hopeful for your future.

KHADIJAH WILLIAMS

Name: Khadijah Williams

From: Brooklyn, NY

Accomplishment: Overcame homelessness to earn top grades and a **scholarship** to Harvard University

Optimists believe a bright future is possible. They focus on what they can do to reach their goals rather than the challenges that may hold them back.

Khadijah Williams was homeless during most of her childhood. This means she and her family did not have a home to live in. Khadijah, her mother, and her younger sister lived in **shelters**, and sometimes had to sleep outside in parks. They moved around a lot in search of places to live. This caused Khadijah to miss a lot of school. She did not stay at one school for long. In fact, she went to twelve different schools in twelve years! Khadijah chose not to focus on the challenges she faced. Instead, she looked for lessons she could learn from her experiences.

Khadijah explains that, "even though I couldn't really control where I would live or anything, I could control how much I wanted to learn." Her hard work and positive attitude helped her earn a scholarship to Harvard University, one of the top universities in the world! She has since graduated and continues to reach for new goals and focus on her bright future.

"To any person, homeless or otherwise, who doesn't like the situation they're in, and feels like they can't do anything about it, they can...For a while, that's all I had—the belief that I could do it. All you need is that belief because you can. I did it."

— Khadijah Williams

This picture shows Khadijah getting ready for her high school graduation while her mother and sister look on.

OPTIMISM AT HOME

Community

School   Home

Self-talk **describes the thoughts we have about ourselves and the situations we face. Self-talk can be negative or positive. A quiet place at home is a good place to practice self-talk.**

Your thoughts are powerful! They affect your actions. Having negative thoughts about yourself or situations you face will make you feel less hopeful. You will be less likely to try to change or improve things. The good news is that you can change your self-talk from negative to positive.

1

Find a quiet place and pay attention to your self-talk. Are your thoughts positive and hopeful, or are they negative and discouraging? Are you being a friend to yourself or a bully?

2

When you catch yourself using negative self-talk, stop and think about how you can change your thoughts to make them more positive.

Situation	Negative Self-Talk	Positive Self-Talk
You and your sister argue about what to watch on T.V.	*"We always fight! We will never get along!"*	*"It's normal for sisters to argue sometimes. If we calm down and listen to each other, I'm sure we can figure this out."*
You fall off your skateboard while learning a new trick.	*"I will never get this right! Why am I so clumsy?"*	*"Even the pros take time to learn new tricks. I will keep trying."*
You ask your brother and his friends to play and they say no.	*"Everyone hates me. I have no friends."*	

Using words like "always," "never," and "everyone" can make a problem seem bigger than it is.

STEP FURTHER

Read the third situation above. Complete the chart by changing the negative self-talk to positive.

OPTIMISM AT SCHOOL

Community

School   Home

A poor mark on a spelling quiz, not doing well on a class presentation, or losing a game in gym class are all examples of setbacks. **It is normal to feel upset when you face them.**

When you feel upset, it is what you do that matters most. Optimistic people look for ways to turn setbacks into success! They think about what they can learn from their mistakes to improve in the future. Positive thinking inspires people to feel hopeful and keep trying when learning something new and challenging.

*Optimistic people believe that setbacks are **temporary**, which means that they will not last. They believe they can improve with hard work.*

STEP FURTHER

Think about a setback you faced at school. How did you find a solution?

When you face a setback, try to keep your mind open to different **solutions**. Talking with teachers, parents, and friends can be helpful. For example, you might ask your teacher for extra spelling work before your next quiz. You could make up spelling games with your friends to study.

OPTIMISM IN YOUR COMMUNITY

Community

School

Home

A community is a group of people who live, work, and play in a place. Your home, school, and neighborhood are part of your community.

Optimists are more likely to try new things, such as getting involved with community events and groups. This is because optimists have **confidence**. When a person has confidence, they believe in themselves and expect they will be successful when they work hard. People who are not confident often avoid trying new things because they expect to fail before they even try.

Optimists try new things and face challenges with an attitude of "I can" instead of "I cannot."

14

Optimists look for ways to improve and grow. They do not compare themselves to others and are not afraid of making mistakes. Optimists know that everyone makes mistakes when trying something new. Getting involved in new activities is a way to make new friends who share your interests. What kinds of groups or clubs are available in your community? Find one that meets your interests. Ask a parent or adult to help you learn more about joining!

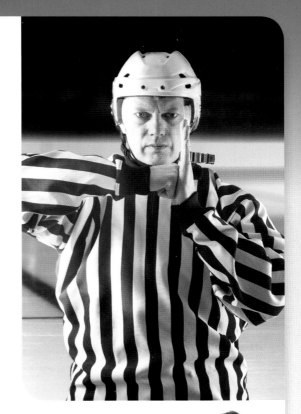

You can build your confidence over time. Joining a group or club in your community can help you discover that you are capable of more than you thought you were!

ROBBY NOVAK

Name: Robby Novak

From: Henderson, TN

Accomplishment: "Kid President" and author, he encourages people to work together to make the world a better place.

Having a positive attitude can make a big difference in your life and in the lives of the people around you! Twelve-year-old Robby Novak is a great example of how one person's positive attitude can encourage others. Robby Novak may be better known as "Kid President."

Since 2012, Robby and his brother-in-law, Brad Montague, have made videos and shared them online. In the videos, Robby as "Kid President" encourages kids and grown-ups to work together to solve problems and make the world a better place. He tells people to celebrate the good things around them. Robby's goal is to "make the world more awesome!" Millions of people have seen Robby's videos. His positive message has spread around the world.

Robby was born with a condition that makes his bones weak and can cause them to easily break. He has had more than 70 broken bones. Robby doesn't let his condition hold him back. He focuses on sharing his positive attitude (and dance moves!) with others.

"You just need to remember: You were born for a reason and you have a purpose—to be awesome and to do awesome things. And you are more capable than you know."

— Robby Novak

Robby tells people to be kind to others by "treating everybody like it's their birthday."

STEP FURTHER

Robby wants people to make the world more awesome. What positive message could you share with others?

FORWARD THINKING

Everyone faces challenges and problems. Sometimes you cannot control the things that happen in your life. One thing you can always control, however, is how you react or respond to the things that happen.

You can always choose to have a positive attitude. By focusing on what you can do to make a situation better, you will feel more in control. Here are some **strategies** that can help you stay positive during challenging times:

"Life is 10% what happens to you and 90% how you react to it."

— Charles R. Swindoll
Writer and speaker

Focus on what is positive in a situation rather than the negative.

Do not let negative things that have happened in the past stop you from trying something today. Focus on what you can do today to be successful in the future.

Think about times when you have overcome challenges. These thoughts can help you feel hopeful. They may also give you ideas for how you can overcome a current challenge.

Optimists believe they have the power to move their lives in positive directions.

STEP FURTHER

What could you say to a friend who wanted to give up on a goal?

PROMOTE POSITIVITY

A role model is someone who acts in a way that sets a good example for others.

Khadijah Williams and Robby Novak are role models who encourage others to live with optimism. You can be a role model to others by showing your positive attitude and sharing what you have learned in this book.

Here are some ways you can promote positivity!

Encourage friends and family to look at setbacks as chances to learn and improve.

Be just as excited about the success of others as you are about your own.

Share stories about positive people and events you hear about in your community and around the world.

Share what you learned about self-talk to help others change their thoughts from negative to positive.

Remind people of their past successes and other times when they have overcome setbacks.

STEPPING FORWARD

Optimism is something you will continue to work on and improve throughout your life.

Use the statements and images below to help you learn about your level of optimism. Use your results to help you find ways you can improve your optimism. There are no right or wrong anwers. Use this page again and again in the future to help make sure you keep stepping forward with optimism!

Read each statement. How well does it describe you?
Think about your recent thoughts and actions to help you decide.

When I make a mistake, I think about what I can learn from it to improve.

I pay attention to my self-talk and try to change negative thoughts into positive thoughts.

I like to try new things and take on challenges.

I stay hopeful and work hard when things do not go well.

I believe that hard work will improve my future.

Very much like me

Somewhat like me

Not like me at all

LEARNING MORE

BOOKS

Meiners, Cheri J. *Be Positive!: A book about optimism.* Free Spirit Publishing, 2013.

Montague, Brad & Robby Novak. *Kid President's Guide to Being Awesome*, HarperCollins, 2015.

Walker, Robert. *Live It: Optimism*, Crabtree Publishing, 2010.

WEBSITES

www.teachertube.com/video/kid-president-pep-talk-281678
This teachertube.com link features a pep talk from Kid President, Robby Novak.

www.embracethefuture.org.au/kids/balloon_game.html
This website includes a game that builds positive thinking patterns as players pop only the balloons with negative messages written on them and let those with positive messages float by.

http://kidshealth.org/en/teens/optimism.html
This link features an article with kid-centered advice for building optimism.

WORDS TO KNOW

condition [k*uh* n-DISH-*uh* n] noun A state of health
confidence [KON-fi-d*uh* ns] noun A belief in one's abilities
 to succeed through hard work
goal [gohl] noun Something that you are trying to do or achieve
negative [neg-uh-tiv] adjective Thinking about the bad
qualities of someone or something
optimist [OP-t*uh*-mist] noun A person who has optimism,
or a positive attitude
pessimist [PES-*uh*-mist] noun A person who has a negative
attitude, or sees the worst in things
positive [POZ-i-tiv] adjective Describing something with an
agreeable or favorable effect
scholarship [SKOL-er-ship] noun Money or aid given to
a student to help them go to school, usually earned by
accomplishments such as high grades
self-talk [self tawk] noun The thoughts and words we tell
ourselves
setback [SET-bak] noun A challenge or stop to progress
shelter [SHEL-ter] noun A building that can be used as a
temporary home for people who are homeless
solutions [s*uh*-LOO-sh*uh* ns] noun Methods or ways of
solving a problem
strategies [STRAT-i-jees] noun Plans for achieving a goal
temporary [TEM-p*uh*-rer-ee] adjective Describing something
that is not permanent or does not last long

INDEX

ABOUT THE AUTHOR

Reagan Miller is an educational consultant,
teacher, and author of more than a dozen
children's books. Researching and writing
this book taught her a lot about optimism
and renewed her positive attitude.

24